# Unsolved!

# MYSTERIES OF ALIEN VISITORS AND ABDUCTIONS

## Kathryn Walker

based on original text by Brian Innes

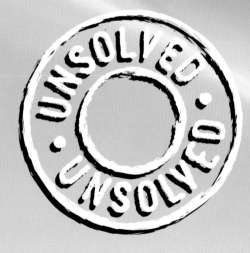

# Crabtree Publishing Company

www.crabtreebooks.com

# Crabtree Publishing Company

## www.crabtreebooks.com

**Author**: Kathryn Walker
  based on original text by Brian Innes
**Project editor**: Kathryn Walker
**Picture researcher**: Rachel Tisdale
**Managing editor**: Miranda Smith
**Art director**: Jeni Child
**Design manager**: David Poole
**Editorial director**: Lindsey Lowe
**Children's publisher**: Anne O'Daly
**Editor**: Molly Aloian
**Proofreaders**: Adrianna Morganelli, Crystal Sikkens
**Project coordinator**: Robert Walker
**Production coordinator**: Katherine Kantor
**Prepress technician**: Katherine Kantor

This edition published in 2009 by
Crabtree Publishing Company

The Brown Reference Group plc
First Floor
9-17 St. Albans Place
London N1 0NX
www.brownreference.com

Copyright © 2008 The Brown Reference Group plc

**Photographs:**
Corbis: Forrest J. Ackerman Collection:
  p. 24–25
Fortean Picture Library: p. 4–5, 14,
  21 (bottom), 22, 23, 28, 29
Istockphoto: Jonas Hamm: p. 11 (bottom);
  David Hughes: p. 16-17;
  Michael Knight: p. 7
Mary Evans Picture Library: p. 8, 12, 18;
  Michael Buhler: p. 13, 21 (top);
  GEOS: p. 19; Billy Meier: p. 27
NASA: p. 26, 30;
  Langley Research Center: p. 9
Science Photo Library:
  Victor Habbick Visions: cover
Shutterstock: Ralf Juergen Kraft: p. 15;
  Iva Villi: p. 11 (top)

Every effort has been made to trace the
owners of copyrighted material.

**Library and Archives Canada Cataloguing in Publication**

Walker, Kathryn, 1957-
    Mysteries of alien visitors and abductions / Kathryn Walker ;
based on original text by Brian Innes.

(Unsolved!)
Includes index.
ISBN 978-0-7787-4141-1 (bound).--ISBN 978-0-7787-4154-1 (pbk.)

    1. Alien abduction--Juvenile literature.  2. Human-alien
encounters--Juvenile literature.  I. Innes, Brian  II. Title.
III. Series: Unsolved! (St. Catharines, Ont.)

BF2050.W34 2008          j001.942          C2008-904325-1

**Library of Congress Cataloging-in-Publication Data**

Walker, Kathryn.
  Mysteries of alien visitors and abductions / Kathryn Walker ; based on original text
by Brian Innes.
      p. cm. -- (Unsolved!)
  Includes index.
  ISBN-13: 978-0-7787-4154-1 (pbk. : alk. paper)
  ISBN-10: 0-7787-4154-0 (pbk. : alk. paper)
  ISBN-13: 978-0-7787-4141-1 (reinforced library binding : alk. paper)
  ISBN-10: 0-7787-4141-9 (reinforced library binding : alk. paper)
  1. Alien abduction--Juvenile literature. 2. Human-alien encounters--Juvenile
literature.  I. Innes, Brian. II. Title.
  BF2050.I55 2009
  001.942--dc22
                                    2008030072

## Crabtree Publishing Company

www.crabtreebooks.com          1-800-387-7650

**Published in Canada**
**Crabtree Publishing**
616 Welland Ave.
St. Catharines, ON
L2M 5V6

**Published in the United States**
**Crabtree Publishing**
PMB16A
350 Fifth Ave., Suite 3308
New York, NY  10118

# Contents

# A Strange Meeting

## ...Betty and Barney Hill said they were kidnapped by aliens.

It was September 19, 1961. The Hills were driving to their home in New Hampshire when they saw a huge aircraft in the sky. Barney said that the aircraft was "like a big pancake."

The Hills were frightened and drove home. But their journey seemed to have taken too long. It was as if two hours had gone missing. Betty started to have nightmares and Barney could not sleep. A doctor used **hypnosis** to try to find out what was causing their problems.

Under hypnosis, Betty and Barney Hill described what had happened in the missing two hours. Their stories matched. Both Barney and Betty said that aliens had taken them into their aircraft. Then the aliens had carried out medical tests on them.

*This picture shows the aircraft that Betty and Barney Hill saw in 1961. Barney stopped the car and got out to take a look at it.*

>> **hypnosis** — When a person is put into a sleep-like state to help them remember things

The doctor who hypnotized the Hills said that the couple believed they were telling the truth.

The same doctor did not think that the Hills really had been kidnapped by aliens. He thought they had imagined the events.

Betty later reported seeing many other UFOs (**Unidentified** Flying Objects).

"Barney said that the aircraft was 'like a big pancake.'"

# Alien Landings

## ...In 1947, hundreds of people reported seeing flying disks.

At first, people named these disks "flying saucers." Later, they became known as UFOs. Some people thought that these were alien spaceships.

In 1947, there were two strange events in New Mexico. Together, they became known as the Roswell Incident. Some people believed the incident was proof that aliens had landed.

First, Mac Brazel found strange **wreckage** on his land. It looked like tinfoil, but it was very tough. Soon afterward, Grady Barnett found more wreckage in the desert. He said it was a metallic, disk-shaped object. He thought it looked like an alien aircraft that had crashed.

Grady said he saw bodies lying beside the wreckage. The bodies were not human.

### How Strange...

- In 1994, the Air Force said that the wreckage found at Roswell had come from a high-flying balloon. They said that the balloon had been used in a secret project.

- The Air Force had been using **test dummies** in their experiments. Grady could have mistaken these for dead aliens.

>> **wreckage** — Fragments of something that has been damaged or destroyed

"Grady said he saw bodies lying beside the wreckage."

In 1947, Grady Barnett said he found a crashed UFO in the desert of New Mexico. This is an artist's idea of what the crash scene may have looked like.

>> **test dummies** — Models of people used in experiments

Over the next few years, there were many UFO sightings. But there was little heard about the creatures inside the UFOs. Then George Adamski reported a meeting.

## Meeting Aliens

George Adamski was a restaurant worker from California. On November 20, 1952, George took a trip into the desert. He said that he saw a UFO and met with an alien from the planet Venus.

George claimed that at other times he had traveled in alien spacecraft. He said he had visited Venus and Mars. He said that he had gone to the far side of Earth's Moon.

*George Adamski wrote this book in 1954. In it, he described his first meeting with aliens in May 1952.*

"...(George Adamski) said he had visited Venus and Mars. He said that he had gone to the far side of Earth's Moon..."

Flying Saucers Have Landed

Desmond Leslie & George Adamski

>> **CIA** — Central Intelligence Agency. This U.S. organization gathers information

## A Changing Story

In 1959, Howard Menger wrote a book about his meetings with aliens. In it, he said he had met aliens from the planets Venus, Mars, and Saturn.

In the early 1960s, Menger admitted that he had lied. He claimed he had been working for the **CIA**. They had used him to help find out how people would **react** to news of UFOs.

In 1967, Menger changed his story again. This time he said that his first story had been true. He claimed that he really had met with aliens.

*This is a photograph of the surface of Mars. It was taken from a module that landed on Mars in 1976. This was part of the Viking 2 space project.*

### How Strange...

• Scientists now know what the far side of Earth's Moon is like. It is not at all as George Adamski described it.

• Space exploration has shown that nothing lives on Venus, Mars, or Earth's Moon.

# Taken by Aliens

## ...Many people say they have been **abducted** by aliens.

Alien abduction is when aliens kidnap people. One of the strangest tales of alien abduction was told by Betty Andreasson.

Betty lived in South Ashburnham, Massachusetts. On January 25, 1967, a reddish light appeared through her kitchen window. Betty's father looked out. He saw a group of strange creatures. Then the family fell into a deep **trance**. Only Betty stayed awake.

The aliens entered Betty's house and took her into their spaceship. The aliens did medical tests on her. They said they were putting secrets in her memory.

Betty's family was still in a trance when she arrived home. The aliens led them all to bed. At first, Betty remembered little of what happened. But nearly ten years later, she told her story under hypnosis.

>> **abducted** — Kidnapped or taken away by force

"The aliens entered Betty's house and took her into their spaceship."

Betty said that the aliens she saw were about four feet (1.2 m) tall. They had gray skin and cat-like eyes. People have often described aliens that look like this.

>> **trance** — A sleep-like state that can be caused by hypnosis

Herbert Schirmer was a policeman. He worked in the town of Ashland, Nebraska. In the early hours of December 3, 1967, Herbert had a strange experience.

"...Herbert wrote up the log of his night's work ... he realized that 25 minutes were missing."

## Lost Time

Herbert was in his patrol car on the outskirts of Ashland. He saw a spacecraft in the road. It was shaped like a huge football and stood on three legs. Red lights were blinking around it. The lights blinked faster and faster. Then the UFO shot out of sight.

Later, Herbert wrote up the **log** of his night's work. As he did this, he realized that 25 minutes were missing. He could not remember what had happened during that time. Herbert had a bad headache and heard weird buzzing sounds in his ears. There was a large, red bruise on his neck.

*This is a photograph of police officer Herbert Schirmer. It was taken in 1967.*

>> **log** — A detailed record of events and the times that they happened

# Inside a UFO

Herbert was asked to try hypnosis. When he did, he told a strange story about the missing 25 minutes. He said that creatures had come out of the UFO. They had narrow heads and cat-like eyes. They were dressed in silver-gray coveralls.

One of the aliens pressed an object to Herbert's neck. It hurt. Then they showed Herbert around the spacecraft. The aliens told him they were from another **galaxy**. They said they had been studying life on Earth for a long time.

The aliens said they would visit Herbert again. Then they took him back to his car.

*This is an artist's idea of a scene in an alien spacecraft. One alien is holding an instrument like the one used on Herbert Schirmer's neck.*

>> **galaxy** — A large system of stars, gas, and dust

On November 5, 1975, Travis Walton was in a forest near Snowflake, Arizona. He was with a woodcutting crew when something very odd happened.

"The beam seemed to throw Travis up into the air."

## Missing for Days

The crew were leaving in their truck when they saw a glowing UFO in the road. Travis walked toward it. The UFO shone a beam of light. The beam seemed to throw Travis up into the air.

The truck driver was terrified and drove off with the rest of the crew. Travis was left alone with the UFO. No one saw him again for five days.

## Fighting Back

Travis turned up in a nearby town. He said he had woken up inside the UFO with three aliens. Travis tried to attack them. Then some humans appeared. One put a mask over Travis' face and he **passed out**. He woke up on the ground as the UFO was taking off.

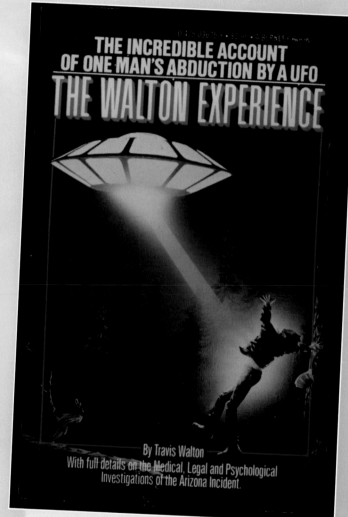

THE INCREDIBLE ACCOUNT OF ONE MAN'S ABDUCTION BY A UFO
THE WALTON EXPERIENCE

By Travis Walton
With full details on the Medical, Legal and Psychological Investigations of the Arizona Incident.

*In 1978, Travis Walton wrote a book about his abduction by aliens.*

>> **passed out** — Fainted or became unconscious

# UFO in New Mexico

On August 13, 1975, Air Force Sergeant Charles L. Moody was in Alamogordo, New Mexico. He was watching the night sky. Suddenly, he saw a disk-shaped UFO coming toward him.

Charles tried to get away but his car would not start. He heard a high-pitched humming noise. Then he felt numb all over. The next thing Charles remembered was the UFO leaving. But more than one hour had passed.

## Guided Tour

During the next two months, Charles began to remember things. He had been aboard the spacecraft. There had been aliens with grayish skin and large heads. They gave Charles a tour of the craft. Then they returned him to his car.

## How Strange...

- The alien leader **communicated** with Charles by passing thoughts into his mind.

- As the UFO left, Charles found that he was able to start his car.

*Charles Moody said that the alien spacecraft he saw was metallic and disk-shaped. Many people claim they have seen UFOs that look like this.*

# Aliens Worldwide

## ...Reports of alien visitors have come from around the world.

Maurice Masse grew **lavender** in Provence, France. On July 1, 1965, Maurice saw a UFO among his lavender bushes. It was shaped like a football and stood on six legs.

Maurice also saw two small figures examining the lavender bushes. But they were not human. They had white skin and huge heads. The aliens saw Maurice and fired something at him. This made him unable to move. Then the aliens returned to their spacecraft and left.

There was proof that something unusual had happened in Maurice's field. A strip of plants had been damaged by heat. Also, there were strange marks in the dirt. Maurice said that these marks were where the UFO had stood.

### How Strange...

- Maurice Masse was not able to grow anything in the area where the UFO had landed for years afterward.

- In April 1964, Lonnie Zamorra had seen a **similar** UFO in New Mexico. He also saw two small figures.

>> **lavender** — A sweet-smelling purple flower that is used in perfumes

This is one of many lavender farms in Provence, France. It was in a field like this that Maurice Masse saw a UFO and two aliens in 1965.

An earlier report of a meeting with aliens came from a village near Arezzo in Italy.

## Laughing Aliens

It was November 1, 1954. Rosa Lotti-Danielli was walking to the village church. She was carrying a bunch of flowers. Suddenly Rosa saw a strange-looking spacecraft. She said it was shaped like two **cones** joined together.

Two creatures appeared. They were about four feet (1.2 m) tall. Rosa could not understand the language that they spoke.

The creatures were laughing and looked friendly. One grabbed Rosa's flowers. He tried to give her something in return. But Rosa was terrified and ran away.

Later, Rosa returned to the spot with the police. There was no sign of the UFO, but other people said that they had seen it, too.

*This picture appeared on a newspaper cover in 1954. It shows Rosa Lotti-Danielli's meeting with the two little aliens.*

>> **cone** — An object that is circular at the bottom and narrows to a point at the top

## A Deadly Meeting?

Inácio de Souza was a farmer. He and his wife lived on a ranch in Pilar de Goiás, Brazil. On August 13, 1967, they saw a huge, disk-shaped spacecraft. It was on the **airstrip** next to the ranch. Next to the spacecraft were three small figures.

"Inácio was frightened. He fired his gun at one of the three figures."

They were wearing tight yellow clothes. The figures ran toward the couple. Inácio was frightened. He fired his gun at one of the three figures. Then a beam of green light shone from the UFO. It struck Inácio and he fell to the ground. The figures ran to the craft. It took off.

Inácio became seriously ill. He died two months later. No one knows for sure if the green light had anything to do with his illness.

*This is an artist's idea of the scene at Pilar de Goiás, in 1967. Inácio de Souza sent his wife indoors before firing his gun.*

# Weird Aliens

...Most aliens are said to have **human-like** forms. But some look very different.

Elmer Sutton and his family lived on a farm near Hopkinsville, Kentucky. On the night of August 21, 1955, the Suttons had friends visiting. The Taylor family had come to stay.

The dog started barking in the yard. Elmer and Billy Ray Taylor grabbed their guns and went outside. A shining figure moved toward them. They shot at it, but the bullets seemed to bounce off it. Then more creatures came.

They were about three feet (91 cm) high with big, yellow eyes. Their ears were huge and flappy. The tiny creatures surrounded the farmhouse. They peeped inside at the terrified families.

The police were called. But when they arrived, they found nothing. The creatures returned later on and finally left at about 5:15 A.M.

## How Strange...

- Elmer and Billy Ray said that the aliens had silvery bodies. They looked as if they were lit from the inside.

- Shooting at the aliens seemed to make their small bodies **glow** brighter.

>> **human-like** — Similar in appearance to a human being

# "The tiny creatures surrounded the farmhouse..."

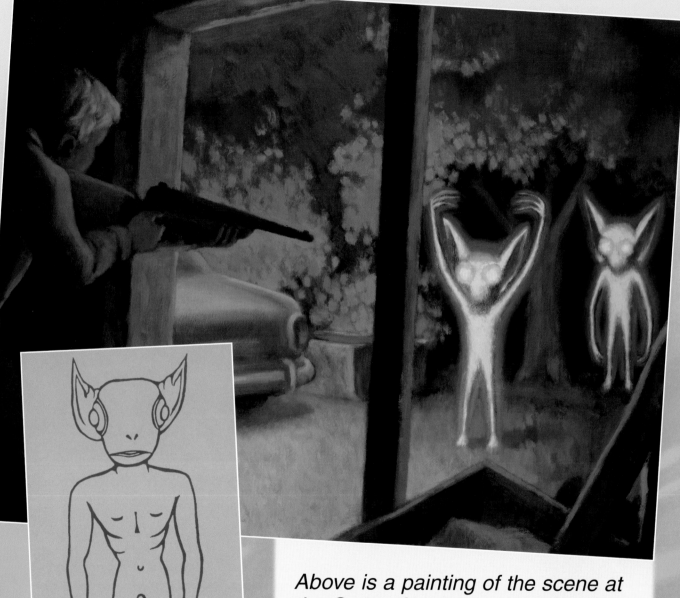

Above is a painting of the scene at the Sutton farmhouse on August 21, 1955. Left is a drawing of one of the aliens seen there.

One of the weirdest reports of an alien life form came from John Hodges of Los Angeles.

## Giant Brains

In August 1971, John was driving his friend, Peter Rodriguez, home. They saw two objects in the road. These looked like enormous human brains. Each was almost three feet (91 cm) high. They appeared to be alive!

John drove around the objects and took his friend home. Then he drove on to his own apartment. But when John arrived home, it was as if two hours had gone missing.

Years later, John went under hypnosis. He remembered more about that night in 1971. The brains had been waiting for him outside his apartment. John believed that one of the brains communicated with him through thought. The brain warned John of the dangers of **nuclear war**.

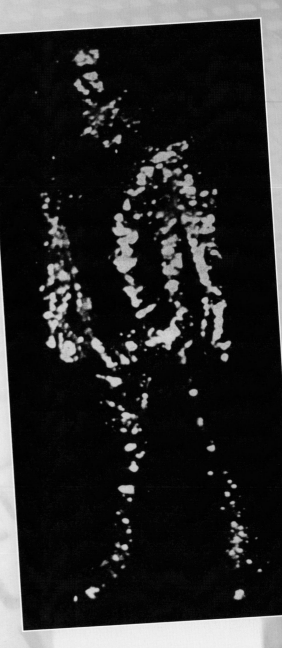

*In 1973, police chief Jeff Greenshaw took this photograph of a silvery figure. He said it was walking away from a UFO.*

>> **nuclear war** — A war in which weapons are used that cause great destruction

## Dog-like Aliens

A very diferent type of alien was reported in 1958 near Depew in New York. A motorist saw two dog-like creatures floating out of a UFO. They had four legs and a tail. They also had two **feelers** under their heads.

## The Pascagoula Aliens

On October 11, 1973, Charles Hickson and Calvin Parker said they were abducted by strange-looking aliens. This happened when they were fishing in the Pascagoula River in Mississippi.

The aliens had bullet-shaped heads and no eyes. Instead of noses and ears, there were thin, spiky objects. The men said these stuck out "like carrots from a snowman's head." The aliens' skin was gray and wrinkled, like an elephant's skin. They seemed to float through the air.

*This is a drawing of one of the aliens that Charles Hickson and Calvin Parker saw in October 1973.*

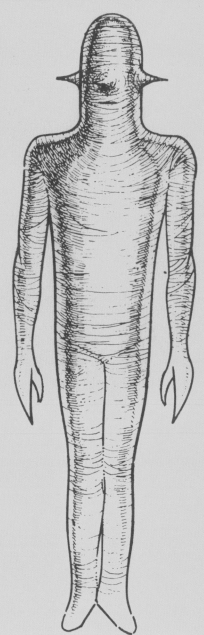

"The aliens had bullet-shaped heads and no eyes."

# What Is the Truth?

## ...Should we believe stories about aliens?

Reports of alien visitors and abductions are often similar. Many people say they cannot remember much at first. They have to be hypnotized to remember what happened.

But similarities with other stories does not mean that a report is true. People who make up stories may use details from older reports. They can use ideas from books, magazines, or movies. They do this because they think it makes their stories more **believable**.

Also, what someone remembers under hypnosis may not be true. Some questions are likely to produce a particular answer. For example, a hypnotist may ask: "Are the eyes cat-like?" The person under hypnosis may not be able to remember. So they are likely to answer "yes."

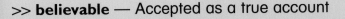

>> **believable** — Accepted as a true account

This picture shows **robots** from another planet attacking Earth. It is a scene from the book War of the Worlds, written by H. G. Wells in 1898.

People have been reporting meetings with aliens for more than 60 years. In the 1950s, the aliens were said to come from the Moon, Mars, or Venus.

## Where Could They Come From?

But space exploration has found that there are no aliens living on these planets. Today, people say that the aliens come from unknown planets.

If this is true, then aliens must come from planets that are hundreds of light-years away from Earth. A light-year is the distance a beam of light can travel in one year. That is about six **trillion** miles! Scientists keep trying to find a way of making space travel faster. But some think it will never be possible to travel at the speed of light.

"In the 1950s, the aliens were said to come from the Moon..."

*This photograph was taken on July 20, 1969. It shows U.S. astronaut Buzz Aldrin walking on Earth's Moon.*

>> **trillion** — One thousand billion, or a million million

*This picture of a UFO was taken by Billy Meier in 1975. It was later found to be a **fake**.*

## Fakes!

Some stories of UFOs and aliens have been proved to be untrue. One story involved a farmer named Billy Meier. Billy lived in the region of Zurich, Switzerland. In 1975, he said he had seen a UFO and met an alien. This alien came from a distant group of stars.

Billy claimed he had met with other aliens, too. He said he had taken hundreds of photographs of UFOs. Then some experts used a computer to test Billy's photographs. They decided that the photographs were fakes.

### How Strange...

- Billy Meier said that his first contact with aliens was in 1942, when he was five years old.

- Billy claimed he met regularly with aliens from the group of stars named the Pleiades.

>> **fake** — Something that is not what it seems to be, but is intended to trick people

Science fiction magazines became popular in the U.S. in the 1920s. These magazines were full of stories about adventures in other worlds. Often, the aliens were similar to humans. But their skin was a different color. Some were described as "little green men."

## Little Green Men

The idea behind these stories may go back centuries. Long before people talked about space travel, they believed in little green men.

Different countries had different names for these small creatures. They were known as pixies, leprechauns, and goblins. If someone disappeared mysteriously, people would say they had been "stolen by the little people."

"Long before people talked about space travel, they believed in little green men."

The creature in this picture is a hobgoblin. In **folktales**, hobgoblins like to play tricks and cause trouble.

*In some folktales, people who dance with the little people are taken to another land. In this picture, a man is being pulled back by his friends before he is taken.*

# Folktales Across the World

There are many folktales about people who are taken to another land by "the little people." Sometimes these people return home. They think they have been gone for a few hours. Instead, hundreds of years have passed. In some ways, these tales are like stories of alien abduction.

People around the world tell the same types of folktales. They all have stories of monsters and mysterious events. We call these stories **myths**.

Many believe that myths develop because they have special meanings to humans. If this is true, then maybe stories of UFOs and alien abductions are myths for modern times.

## How Strange...

- In folktales, goblins can be playful and sometimes evil.

- Pixies are often said to have green skin and pointed ears. People who follow them may disappear forever.

>> **myth** — An ancient story, often about heroes and beings that are not human

What is the truth? Do aliens really exist and could they be visiting Earth?

## Looking for Aliens

Space exploration has not found aliens living in our **solar system**. But we do not know if there is life on more distant planets. Some scientists are working to find out if there is anyone out there. They are sending radio signals into space. They are also listening for signals from space.

If there are aliens, they would have to travel huge distances to visit us. In books and movies, spaceships travel to distant planets. In real life, humans have not found a way to do this.

## A Trick of the Mind?

Some people really believe that they have met or been abducted by aliens. It is possible that these people have false memories. These are memories that seem real, but have been imagined or changed in some way.

There are many reasons to doubt reports of alien visitors. But the truth is that we do not know if aliens exist somewhere in outer space.

"...scientists are working to find out if there is anyone out there."

*This is part of the Goldstone Tracking Station in southern California. It has equipment that listens for signals from outer space.*

>> **solar system** — The Sun and the planets that move around it

# Glossary

**abducted** Kidnapped or taken away by force

**airstrip** A runway where aircraft can take off and land

**believable** Accepted as a true account

**CIA** Central Intelligence Agency. This U.S. organization gathers information

**communicate** Pass on or make known information, thoughts, or feelings

**cone** An object that is circular at the bottom and narrows to a point at the top

**fake** Something that is not what it seems to be, but is intended to trick people

**feelers** Movable parts that are used to touch things

**folktales** Old stories that are passed down from generation to generation

**galaxy** A large system of stars, gas, and dust

**glow** To shine steadily with a soft light

**human-like** Similar in appearance to a human being

**hypnosis** When a person is put into a sleep-like state to help them remember things

**lavender** A sweet-smelling purple flower that is used in perfumes

**log** A detailed record of events and the times that they happened

**myth** An ancient story, often about heroes and beings that are not human

**nuclear war** A war in which weapons are used that cause great destruction

**passed out** Fainted or became unconscious

**react** To act in response to something or someone

**robot** A machine that can perform many of the tasks that a human does

**similar** Having qualities in common

**solar system** The Sun and the planets that move around it

**test dummies** Models of people used in experiments

**trance** A sleep-like state that can be caused by hypnosis

**trillion** One thousand billion, or a million million

**unidentified** When you do not know what something is

**wreckage** Fragments of something that has been damaged or destroyed

# Index

# Further Reading

- Deary, Terry. *Alien Landing*, "Classified" series. Kingfisher, 2004.
- Herbst, Judith. *Aliens*, "The Unexplained" series. Lerner Publications, 2004.
- Orme, David. *UFOs: Are They Real?* "Trailblazers" series. Ransom, 2007.
- Roleff, Tamara. *Alien Abductions*, "Fact or Fiction" series. Greenhaven Press, 2003.
- Tiger, Caroline. *The UFO Hunter's Handbook*, "Field Guides to the Paranormal" series. Price Stern Sloan, 2001.

Printed in the U.S.A.